THE BEST 50
CREPE RECIPES

Coleen and Bob Simmons

BRISTOL PUBLISHING ENTERPRISES
San Leandro, California

Printed in the United States of America.

ISBN 1-55867-113-7

Cover design: Frank Paredes
Cover photography: John Benson
Food stylist: Suzanne Carreiro

ABOUT CREPES

A crepe is just a very thin pancake that uses only eggs for leavening. Crepes can easily be rolled around a filling or folded and stuffed, or they can be sauced and served without a stuffing.

Because of their association with French cooking, crepes have had the reputation for being mysterious and complicated. Actually they are easy to produce. The difference between a pancake and a crepe is primarily consistency. Crepes are made as thin as possible so they can be rolled or folded around a filling, while pancakes tend to be puffier and more substantial. Crepes can be wrapped around delicious combinations of vegetables, fish, poultry or meat and topped with a sauce for luncheon or dinner entrées, or they can be filled with yesterday's leftover chicken and covered with a simple sauce for a quick dinner entrée on a busy day.

Crepes for dessert are elegant and appropriate for almost any occasion. Best of all for these busy days, they are easy to serve. While they may require some last-minute preparation or heating, the crepes, filling and sauce can be made in advance so the final

step never takes long. You can make one of the delicious recipes in this book, or you can simply fill crepes with jam and sprinkle with powdered sugar, or fill them with ice cream and top with your favorite sauce.

CREPES FOR THE 90s

Because today's trend is toward lighter and healthier foods, we have streamlined several of the classic rich crepe sauces. Some delicious and less calorific crepe toppings include a little grated Parmesan cheese, or a light brushing of olive oil sprinkled with toasted sesame seeds. Some crepes are delicious served with only a tomato salsa, mango chutney or *Yogurt Cucumber Sauce* on the side for a flavor punch. There are several meatless crepe fillings that make a substantial entrée or can be used to fill smaller crepes and served as a vegetable side dish for grilled or roasted meats.

Make a crepe batter and cook the crepes when you have a few minutes, and then cover and refrigerate them. They will keep well for several days and be ready for filling on a moment's notice.

CLASSIC CREPES

Here is a terrific basic crepe recipe with general cooking instructions.

2 eggs
2 tbs. melted butter or vegetable oil
1⅓ cups milk
1 cup all-purpose flour
½ tsp. salt

Place ingredients in a blender or food processor, cover and process for 20 to 30 seconds. Scrape down sides of container and process for a few more seconds. Crepe batter can be used immediately, or refrigerated until needed. If it thickens on standing, thin to the right consistency with a little milk. Crepe batter should be thin enough to run freely around the bottom of the crepe pan when it is tilted.

Makes 14-16 crepes (6-inch) or 18-22 crepes (5-inch)

If not using a blender or food processor: Beat eggs, butter or oil and milk with a rotary egg beater or electric mixer until blended. Gradually add dry ingredients and beat until smooth. To be sure batter is completely smooth, pour it through a coarse sieve to catch any lumps which may not have dissolved. Refrigerate batter for about 2 hours before cooking.

To prepare the pan: Use a well-seasoned 6- or 7-inch nonstick pan, measured across the bottom, or a small skillet for entrée crepes, or a 5- or 6-inch pan for dessert crepes. Spray pan with nonstick cooking spray. Before cooking the first crepe, add ½ tsp. butter to the pan.

Pan temperature: The crepe pan is at the correct temperature when the batter sizzles slightly when poured into the pan. A crepe will cook on one side in about 1 minute. Crepes should be flecked with light brown and flexible, but still pale in color.

To cook crepes: Two or three tablespoons of batter is usually enough to evenly coat the entire bottom of a 6- or 7-inch crepe pan. If necessary, adjust the amount of batter needed for the pan

you are using. Pour in the batter and quickly tilt the pan so the batter entirely covers the bottom. If you have put in more than just a thin coating, pour the excess back into the bowl. This will leave a small flap on the crepe but it won't be noticed when the crepe is filled and folded. It is important to have the pan at the correct temperature before starting to cook.

To turn crepe: The crepe is ready to turn when it begins to set and begins to look dry or crisp around the edges. Loosen around the edge with a spatula or knife so you have a starting place to pick up the crepe with your fingers, and then simply flip it over. If you prefer, carefully turn with a spatula. Should it start to tear when picked up, it may not be cooked enough to turn. Cook for a few seconds longer and try again.

If pan sticks in one spot: Put more butter or oil in the pan and wipe with a paper towel. Once a crepe pan is seasoned, it should not be necessary to add more butter or oil for each crepe. It may be necessary to discard the first crepe or two until the pan is properly seasoned and the temperature is correct. Once a metal

pan is seasoned, never wash or scrub it. Wipe with a paper towel and don't use the pan for anything else or you must season it each time it is used. A nonstick pan does not have to be seasoned.

After the crepes are cooked, stack them on a plate. They will be easier to separate if they are not placed squarely on top of each other. It is not necessary to put foil or waxed paper between each crepe. If crepes are made ahead and chilled, however, the butter or oil will cause them to stick together, so bring them to room temperature or warm them slightly in the oven or microwave in order to separate them easily.

To store: Crepes will keep several days in the refrigerator. Wrap them in foil or plastic.

To freeze: Crepes to be frozen can be stacked right on a piece of foil large enough to be folded over the crepes and tightly sealed. Place foil package in a plastic bag and freeze until needed. It is not necessary to put foil or waxed paper between each crepe. They will pull apart easily when they are defrosted and warmed slightly. Package crepes in the number you will need for a meal, allowing

two 6-inch crepes per serving. If using small ones for main dish crepes, allow three per serving. Two 5-inch crepes per serving is enough for desserts unless otherwise specified. Filled crepes do not freeze well in most cases. Freeze crepes and fillings separately.

To defrost: A foil package of 6 to 8 crepes will defrost in a 350° oven in 8 to 10 minutes. If planning to defrost in the microwave, wrap the crepes in plastic wrap or store in a microwavable dish. Use the DEFROST setting for 2 minutes, repeating as necessary for the number of crepes being defrosted. Carefully separate crepes while they are still warm.

Your crepes will improve with practice. Crepes that are not perfectly round or that have holes will never be noticed when they are filled, rolled and covered with sauce.

To serve: The first side is the most attractive. Place crepes on the plate pretty side down, ready to fill or fold. Crepes can be filled and rolled in a number of ways. See illustrations on page 8.

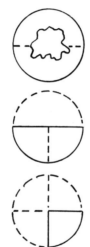

**CLASSIC
CREPE ROLL**

**CREPE
TRIANGLES**

BLINTZES

MAKING CREPES

BUTTERMILK CREPES

Buttermilk and cake flour make these very tender and give them a tang.

2 eggs
2 tbs. vegetable oil or melted butter
1 cup buttermilk
1/3 cup water
1/2 cup sifted cake flour
1/2 cup all-purpose flour
1/2 tsp. salt

Place ingredients in a blender or food processor and process for 20 to 30 seconds until well combined. Scrape down sides of container and process for a few more seconds. Cook according to directions beginning on page 3.

Makes 14-16 crepes (6-inch)

NO CHOLESTEROL CREPES

Egg Beaters or other cholesterol-free egg substitutes can be used to make a delicious tender crepe. It may be necessary to occasionally wipe the pan with a little oil or margarine if crepes start to stick.

4 oz. Egg Beaters
3 tbs. vegetable oil or melted margarine
1⅓ cups milk
1 cup all-purpose flour
½ tsp. salt

Place ingredients in a blender or food processor and process for 20 to 30 seconds until well combined. Scrape down sides of container and process for a few more seconds. Cook according to directions beginning on page 3.

Makes 14-16 crepes (6-inch)

CORN CHIP CREPES

These resemble a tender corn tortilla and are delicious with Mexican-style fillings.

2 eggs
2 tbs. vegetable oil
1 cup milk
1/3 cup water
1/2 cup all-purpose flour
1 cup loosely-packed, crushed Fritos corn chips
1/2 tsp. salt

Place all ingredients in a blender or food processor, cover and process for 20 to 30 seconds. Scrape down sides of container and blend for a few more seconds until mixture is very smooth. Cook according to directions beginning on page 3. Stir batter occasionally to prevent corn chips from settling to the bottom.

Makes 14-16 crepes (6-inch)

SPINACH CREPES

These flavorful crepes have a pretty deep green color. Fill them with any creamy filling.

¼ cup cooked spinach, drained
2 eggs
1½ cups milk
2 tbs. vegetable oil, or melted butter
1 cup all-purpose flour
½ tsp. salt

3 green onions, chopped, or 1 tbs. minced chives
¼ tsp. dried thyme, or 1 tsp. fresh thyme leaves
dash white pepper
dash nutmeg

Squeeze cooked spinach until very dry and chop. Place eggs, milk, oil or butter, flour and salt in a blender or food processor. Cover and process until thoroughly combined. Add spinach and remaining ingredients; process for 20 to 30 seconds longer. Cook according to directions beginning on page 3.

Makes 14-16 crepes (6-inch)

WHOLE WHEAT CREPES

For brunch, serve with **Curried Egg** *filling, page 44, or*
Spinach and Ricotta *filling, page 50, and a fresh fruit compote.*

2 eggs
2 tbs. vegetable oil
1⅓ cups milk
1 tbs. honey
½ cup whole wheat flour
½ cup all-purpose flour
½ tsp. salt

Place ingredients in a blender or food processor, cover and process for 20 to 30 seconds. Scrape down sides of container and blend for a few more seconds until mixture is quite smooth. Cook according to directions beginning on page 3.

Makes 14-16 crepes (6-inch)

CANNELLONI OR MANICOTTI CREPES

These are more substantial crepes and make great substitutes for pasta squares.

2 eggs
¾ cup water
¾ cup all-purpose flour
¼ tsp. salt

Place ingredients in a blender or food processor, cover and process for 20 to 30 seconds. Scrape down sides of container and blend for a few more seconds. Cook crepes in a 6- or 7-inch pan according to directions beginning on page 3.

Makes 8 crepes

CLASSIC DESSERT CREPES

Sweet dessert crepes make a great dinner party finale. Fill them with fresh fruit, or smear them with jam, fold and sprinkle with powdered sugar. Allow 2 crepes per serving.

2 eggs
2 tbs. melted butter
1¼ cups milk
2 tbs. brandy, or orange liqueur
1 tbs. sugar
1 cup sifted cake flour
½ tsp. salt

Place ingredients in a blender or food processor, cover and process for 20 to 30 seconds until well combined. Scrape down sides of container and process for a few more seconds. Cook according to directions beginning on page 3.

Makes 16-20 crepes (5-inch)

CHOCOLATE CREPES

Created for chocolate lovers, these are delicious when filled with ice cream.

2 eggs
1 tbs. melted butter
1 oz. melted semisweet
  chocolate
1 tbs. cocoa
1 1/4 cups milk

1/2 tsp. vanilla extract
1/2 tsp. chocolate extract
1/4 cup sugar
1 cup all-purpose flour
dash of salt
dash of cinnamon

Place ingredients in a blender or food processor and process for 20 to 30 seconds. Scrape down sides of container and process for a few more seconds. Cook crepes according to directions beginning on page 3.

Makes 20-24 crepes (5-inch)

ORANGE DESSERT CREPES

*Use for **Crepes Suzette**, page 68, or fill with orange sherbet for a delicious dessert.*

3 eggs
2 tbs. melted butter
$\frac{1}{4}$ cup frozen orange juice concentrate, undiluted
1 cup milk
1 tbs. Triple Sec, or Cointreau
1 cup flour
2 tbs. sugar
dash salt

Place ingredients in a blender or food processor and process for 20 to 30 seconds. Scrape down sides of container and process for a few more seconds. Cook according to directions beginning on page 3.

Makes 18-22 crepes (5-inch)

SOUR CREAM DESSERT CREPES

*These delicate crepes make a lovely light finish to a meal. Fill them with fresh raspberries and whipped cream, or **Lemon Meringue** filling, page 73.*

2 eggs
2 tbs. melted butter or
  vegetable oil
1 cup sour cream
1/2 cup milk

1 cup sifted cake flour
2 tbs. sugar
2 tbs. brandy
dash salt

Place ingredients in blender or food processor and process for 20 to 30 seconds. Scrape down sides of container and process for a few more seconds. Cook according to directions beginning on page 3.

Makes 18-22 crepes (5-inch)

WALNUT DESSERT CREPES

*Serve with strawberries or peaches and whipped cream for a perfect summertime dessert, or **Chestnut Rum** filling, page 65, for a great fall or holiday treat.*

2 eggs
2 tbs. vegetable oil or melted
  butter
1¼ cups milk
1 tbs. honey

1 tbs. cream sherry, or brandy
¾ cup flour
½ cup coarsely chopped
  walnuts
dash salt

Place ingredients in a blender or food processor and process for 20 to 30 seconds. Scrape down sides of container and blend a few more seconds. Cook crepes according to directions beginning on page 3.

Makes 18-22 crepes (5-inch)

SAVORY CHEESE CREPE TRIANGLES

Serve in place of a cheese course with a glass of red wine, or accompany with a crisp green salad for lunch.

8 *Classic Crepes*, page 3
2 tbs. butter
2 tbs. flour
1 cup milk

white pepper to taste
1/3 cup crumbled blue, Roque-
fort or Gorgonzola cheese
4 egg whites, stiffly beaten

Make crepes. Preheat oven to 350°. Melt butter in a small saucepan. Add flour and cook 2 minutes. Gradually add milk and white pepper. Cook, stirring, until sauce thickens. Remove from heat and stir in cheese. Allow to cool for 5 minutes before folding in eggs. Fill crepes and fold into triangles (see illustration on page 8). Bake for about 20 minutes, or until filling is puffed. If crepes brown too quickly, turn oven temperature down. Remove to individual serving plates. Serve immediately.

Makes 8 crepe triangles

ASPARAGUS AND HAM CREPES

Serve this elegant entrée when asparagus is in season.

8 *Classic Crepes*, page 3
1½ tbs. Dijon mustard
8 thin slices ham
16 cooked asparagus spears
1½ cups grated Swiss cheese
2 tbs. butter

2-3 green onions, white part only, finely chopped
2 tbs. flour
1¼ cups milk
¼ tsp. white pepper
salt to taste

Make crepes. Preheat oven to 375°. Lightly coat one side of each crepe with mustard and top with 1 slice ham. Place 2 asparagus spears and 2 tbs. cheese on top of ham. Roll up and place seam side down in a buttered ovenproof serving dish. Melt butter in a small saucepan and sauté onions for 1 to 2 minutes. Add flour and cook 2 minutes. Gradually add milk and cook, stirring, over low heat until sauce thickens. Stir in remaining ½ cup cheese, pepper and salt. Spoon sauce over crepes. Heat in oven for 10 to 15 minutes. Broil to brown lightly. Serve immediately.

Makes 4 servings

MUSHROOM AND HAM CREPES

*This also makes a terrific filling for **Spinach Crepes**, page 12, or **Whole Wheat Crepes**, page 13. Use the brown Italian or Crimini mushrooms if you can find them.*

8 *Buttermilk Crepes*, page 9
¼ cup butter
1 lb. fresh mushrooms, coarsely chopped
¼ cup finely minced shallots, or green onions
1 cup finely chopped ham, about 4 oz.
salt and white pepper
¼ cup minced fresh parsley
1 cup light sour cream
Creamy Mustard Sauce, page 23

Make crepes. Preheat oven to 350°. Melt butter in a large skillet and sauté mushrooms over high heat for 3 to 4 minutes. Add shallots, lower heat and cook for 2 to 3 minutes. Add chopped ham, salt and pepper. Cook a few more minutes until mixture is

dry. Fold in parsley and sour cream just before assembling crepes. Spread filling on crepes, roll up and place in a buttered ovenproof serving dish. Heat in oven for 10 to 15 minutes. Top with *Creamy Mustard Sauce* and serve immediately.

Makes 4 servings

CREAMY MUSTARD SAUCE

1 tbs. butter or margarine
1 tbs. flour
1¼ cups milk
1 tbs. Dijon mustard

1 tsp. Worcestershire sauce
salt and freshly ground pepper
dash nutmeg

Melt butter or margarine in a small saucepan, add flour and cook for 2 minutes, mixing well. Gradually add milk and cook, stirring, over low heat until mixture comes to a boil and starts to thicken. Stir in remaining ingredients and cook for another 1 to 2 minutes. Makes 1¼ cups.

BLACK BEAN AND CHICKEN CREPES

This hearty entrée goes together quickly.

8-10 *Corn Chip Crepes*, page 11, or *Classic Crepes*, page 3
1 tbs. vegetable oil
1 large clove garlic, minced
2 cans (15 oz. each) black beans, drained
1½ cups diced cooked chicken
6-8 drops hot pepper sauce, optional
½ cup sour cream
fresh cilantro leaves for garnish

Make crepes. Preheat oven to 375°. Heat oil in a medium skillet. Sauté garlic over low heat for 2 to 3 minutes. Place drained beans in a food processor and process until smooth. Add bean puree and chicken to garlic; add hot pepper sauce if desired. Cook, stirring, over medium heat until well combined. Divide mixture among crepes and fold into triangles or roll up. Place in an oiled ovenproof serving dish or individual dishes and heat in oven for 10 to 12 minutes until lightly browned. Place a dollop of sour cream on each crepe, top with fresh cilantro leaves and serve.

Makes 4-5 servings

CHICKEN AND GREEN CHILE CREPES

Accent these with some fresh prepared salsa on the side.

8 *Corn Chip Crepes*, page 11
½ tsp. ground cumin
¾ cup sour cream
2 cups cubed cooked chicken
1 canned green chile, seeded,
  chopped, about ¼ cup

2 tbs. chopped pimiento, or
  roasted red pepper pieces
¼ cup minced fresh cilantro
  leaves
salt and freshly ground pepper
¾ cup grated Monterey Jack
  cheese

Make crepes. Preheat oven to 375°. Combine cumin with sour cream in a medium mixing bowl. Add remaining ingredients, except Monterey Jack cheese, and mix well. Spoon a little mixture on each crepe and roll. Place filled crepes in a buttered ovenproof serving dish or individual dishes. Sprinkle with grated cheese and heat in oven for about 10 minutes. Broil to brown lightly. Serve immediately.

Makes 4 servings

CHICKEN AND BROCCOLI CREPES

Classic Chicken Divan wrapped in crepes makes a party entrée.

8 *Classic Crepes*, page 3
3 tbs. butter or margarine
2 tbs. minced shallot
2 cloves garlic, minced
3 tbs. flour
2 cups milk
dash dried red pepper flakes
2 tsp. Worcestershire sauce
1 cup grated sharp cheddar cheese
salt and freshly ground pepper
2 cups cubed cooked chicken
8 pieces cooked broccoli, cut in half lengthwise
grated Parmesan cheese

Make crepes. Preheat oven to 375°. Melt butter or margarine in a small saucepan and cook shallots and garlic over low heat for 1 to 2 minutes. Add flour and cook, stirring, for 2 minutes. Gradually add milk and cook until mixture thickens. Add red pepper flakes, Worcestershire, grated cheese, salt and pepper. Remove ½ cup sauce. Stir chicken pieces into sauce. Divide chicken mixture among crepes. Arrange 2 pieces of broccoli on each crepe so that florets will be showing on each end when crepe is rolled. Place rolled crepes seam side down in a buttered, oven-proof serving dish. Spoon reserved sauce over crepes and sprinkle with Parmesan cheese. Heat in oven for 10 to 15 minutes and broil to brown lightly. Serve immediately.

Makes 4 servings

CURRIED CHICKEN CREPES

Cooked chicken and crunchy jicama-filled crepes are sauced with a light vegetable curry. Serve with chutney or fruit salad.

8 *Whole Wheat Crepes*, page 13, or *Corn Chip Crepes*, page 11
2 tbs. butter or margarine
1 small onion, coarsely chopped
1 small carrot, peeled, finely chopped
2 tsp. curry powder
1 tart green apple, peeled, coarsely chopped
1 can (14½ oz.) chicken stock
2 tsp. cornstarch dissolved in 1 tbs. cold water
2 cups diced cooked chicken
2 cups peeled, diced jicama
½ cup raisins
½ cup coarsely chopped dry roasted, unsalted peanuts
for garnish
¼ cup finely chopped fresh cilantro for garnish

Make crepes. Preheat oven to 375°. Melt butter in a medium skillet. Sauté onion and carrot for 4 to 5 minutes over low heat. Add curry powder and cook for 1 to 2 minutes. Add apple pieces and chicken stock. Cover and simmer for about 12 to 15 minutes until vegetables are soft. Add dissolved cornstarch to skillet and bring to a boil. Pour vegetables into a food processor or blender and process until smooth. Combine cooked chicken, jicama and raisins. Add 1 cup vegetable sauce and mix well. Fill crepes with chicken mixture and place in a buttered ovenproof serving dish. Top with remaining sauce. Bake for 10 to 12 minutes until hot. Garnish with peanuts and cilantro.

Makes 4 servings

CHILE VERDE

Pork and green chiles make a zesty supper dish.

12 *Corn Chip Crepes*, page 11
1 tbs. butter
½ cup finely chopped onion
2 cups cubed cooked pork
1 can (4 oz.) diced green chiles with juice
1 tsp. salt
¼ tsp. freshly ground pepper
¾ cup water
1 tbs. melted butter combined with
1 tbs. flour for thickening
3-4 drops hot pepper sauce
grated Monterey Jack cheese for garnish
fresh cilantro leaves for garnish

Make crepes. Heat oven to 375°. Melt butter in a skillet and sauté onion until soft. Add cooked pork, chiles and juice, salt, pepper and water. Bring to a boil, cover and simmer over medium heat for 25 to 30 minutes until mixture has thickened slightly. Blend melted butter and flour together. Taste pork mixture and add hot pepper sauce, if desired. Gradually stir in a little butter-flour mixture to sauce to thicken. Spoon some filling on each crepe and roll. Place filled crepes in a buttered ovenproof serving dish or individual dishes and pour any remaining filling over crepes. Sprinkle with cheese and heat in oven for 10 to 15 minutes. Broil until lightly brown. Top with cilantro leaves and serve immediately.

Makes 6 servings

CREPES A LA STROGANOFF

Steak with a creamy mushroom sauce makes a very delicious and satisfying entrée. Serve with a crunchy grated carrot or cabbage salad.

8 *Classic Crepes*, page 3, or *Whole Wheat Crepes*, page 13
1 lb. round steak, or small flank steak
½ lb. fresh mushrooms
4 tbs. butter
½ cup chopped onion
2 medium tomatoes, peeled, seeded, chopped
1 clove garlic, minced
salt and freshly ground pepper
1 tbs. Worcestershire sauce
6 drops hot pepper sauce
1¼ cups sour cream

Make crepes. Cut steak into $1/2$-x-1-inch, $1/4$-inch-thick strips. Thinly slice mushrooms and sauté in 2 tbs. butter. Remove from saucepan and set aside. Add remaining butter to saucepan. Brown meat and onion together over high heat, stirring constantly. Add tomatoes, garlic, salt, pepper, Worcestershire and hot pepper sauce to meat. Cover and simmer for 30 to 40 minutes. When meat is tender, stir in 1 cup sour cream and just heat through. Do not boil. Divide mixture among crepes. Roll and place in a buttered ovenproof serving dish. Broil for 2 to 3 minutes to brown lightly. Top each crepe with a spoonful of sour cream and serve immediately.

Makes 4 servings

SCALLOP AND CORN CREPES

Use small bay scallops if you can get them, or cut larger ones into quarters. A tropical fruit salsa or mango chutney makes a delicious accent.

12 *Corn Chip Crepes*, page 11, or *Spinach Crepes*, page 12
3 tbs. butter
2 green onions, thinly sliced
3 tbs. flour
1½ cups milk
½ tsp. grated lemon rind
2 tbs. lemon juice
salt and freshly ground pepper
1 lb. small scallops
1 cup cooked corn
1 large tomato, peeled, seeded, chopped
10-12 fresh basil leaves, shredded

Make crepes. Melt butter in small saucepan and cook onions for 1 to 2 minutes. Add flour and cook for 2 minutes. Gradually add milk and continue cooking until mixture thickens. Stir in lemon rind, juice, salt and pepper. Remove ½ cup sauce and set aside. Add scallops and corn to saucepan and cook for 3 to 4 minutes until scallops start to firm. Fold in tomato pieces and basil. Fill crepes and roll or fold into triangles. Place in buttered, ovenproof serving dishes. Top with reserved sauce and broil until lightly browned. Serve immediately.

Servings: 4-6

SCALLOP AND SPINACH CREPES

Serve these as an elegant appetizer for a special dinner. Make the filling ahead, fill and heat crepes just before serving.

8 *Buttermilk Crepes*, page 9
1/2 lb. small scallops, or large scallops cut into quarters
2 tbs. butter
6-8 medium mushrooms, thinly sliced
3-4 green onions, finely chopped
1 pkg. (10 oz.) frozen spinach, defrosted, squeezed dry
2 tsp. lemon juice

CREAMY CLAM SAUCE

2 tbs. plus 1 tsp. cornstarch
8 oz. clam juice
1/3 cup heavy cream
5-6 drops hot pepper sauce
salt and freshly ground pepper
a little grated nutmeg
grated Parmesan cheese for topping

Make crepes. Preheat oven to 375°.

Prepare scallops: Remove small tough pieces of muscle, rinse well to remove any sand and pat dry. Melt butter in a medium skillet. Sauté mushrooms and onions over medium high heat for 3 to 4 minutes. Chop drained spinach and add to mushrooms with lemon juice. Combine and cook for 1 to 2 minutes.

Prepare sauce: Dissolve cornstarch in a small amount of clam juice in a small saucepan. Add remaining clam juice and cream. Slowly bring to a boil and cook until sauce thickens. Stir in hot pepper sauce, salt, pepper and nutmeg.

Remove $\frac{1}{2}$ cup sauce and set aside. Add scallops to saucepan. Cook for 3 to 4 minutes until scallops start to firm. Add scallops and sauce to mushrooms and mix well. Fill crepes and place in an ovenproof serving casserole or individual serving dishes. Spoon reserved sauce over crepes and top with Parmesan cheese. Bake for 10 to 12 minutes to heat through and lightly brown, or if mixture is hot, broil until lightly browned. Serve immediately.

Makes 3-4 servings

GREEK-STYLE SHRIMP CREPES

Shrimp, tomatoes and feta cheese-filled crepes make a great brunch or supper entrée.

8 *Classic Crepes*, page 3
2 tbs. olive oil
1 cup finely chopped onion
$\frac{1}{2}$ cup finely chopped red bell pepper
$\frac{1}{4}$ cup finely chopped celery
1 clove garlic, minced
$\frac{1}{2}$ cup dry vermouth, or white wine
2 cups peeled, seeded, chopped tomatoes, or 1 can
(14$\frac{1}{2}$ oz.) tomato pieces, drained
$\frac{1}{2}$ tsp. dried thyme
1 tsp. Worcestershire sauce
4-6 drops hot pepper sauce, or to taste
1 lb. small fresh shrimp, shelled, deveined
1 cup crumbled feta cheese, about 5 oz.
salt and freshly ground pepper

Make crepes. Preheat oven to 375°. Heat olive oil in a large skillet and sauté onion, pepper and celery for 8 to 10 minutes. Add garlic, vermouth, tomatoes, thyme, Worcestershire and hot pepper sauce. Cook over fairly high heat for 8 to 10 minutes until mixture thickens. Add shrimp and cook for 1 to 2 minutes until shrimp turns pink. Stir in feta, salt and pepper. Divide shrimp mixture among crepes, reserving 8 shrimp. Roll and place in buttered ovenproof serving dishes. Heat in oven for 10 to 15 minutes until hot and bubbly. A minute or two before serving, place a reserved shrimp on top of each crepe and return to oven briefly.

Makes 4 servings

CURRIED CAULIFLOWER CREPES

Mildly curried vegetables are wrapped in a crepe for a light dinner. Serve a spicy chutney on the side for a delicious accent.

8 *Whole Wheat Crepes,* page 13
1 large cauliflower, about 1½ lb.
2 tbs. butter or margarine
1 cup chopped sweet onions
1 tsp. curry powder
2 tbs. heavy cream
dash hot pepper sauce
salt and freshly ground pepper
1 cup frozen green peas, defrosted
½ cup grated Parmesan cheese
¼ cup finely chopped fresh parsley

Make crepes. Preheat oven to 375°. Cut cauliflower into ½-inch pieces and steam until tender, about 10 minutes. Melt butter or margarine in a small skillet, add onions and cook over low heat until onions are very soft. Add curry powder to onions and cook for another minute. In a food processor or blender, puree 2 cups steamed cauliflower with 2 tbs. heavy cream, hot pepper sauce, salt and pepper. Combine pureed cauliflower with onions, remaining cauliflower pieces and green peas. Fill crepes, roll up and place in a buttered ovenproof serving dish or individual dishes. Sprinkle crepes with Parmesan cheese and heat in oven for 10 minutes. Broil until lightly browned. Sprinkle crepes with fresh chopped parsley and serve immediately.

Makes 4 servings

SHRIMP AND AVOCADO CREPES

These make a terrific summer lunch or supper dish.

8 *Corn Chip Crepes*, page 11
½ cup light cream cheese
2 tsp. lime juice
½ lb. small cooked salad shrimp
1 large tomato, peeled,
  seeded, chopped
2 green onions, white part
  only, finely minced

¼ cup finely chopped fresh
  cilantro
salt and freshly ground pepper
1 large avocado, peeled, cut
  into small cubes
¼ cup grated Parmesan cheese

Make crepes. Preheat oven to 375°. Mix cream cheese with lime juice. Gently mix remaining ingredients, except Parmesan cheese, with cream cheese, folding in avocado last. Spoon shrimp mixture on crepes and roll. Place filled crepes in a buttered, ovenproof serving dish or individual dishes. Sprinkle Parmesan cheese over crepes and heat in oven for about 10 minutes. Broil until lightly browned. Serve immediately.

Makes 4 servings

CORN, PEPPERS AND REFRIED BEAN CREPES

This makes a delicious vegetable entrée, or serve as a side dish.

8 *Corn Chip Crepes*, page 11,
  or *Classic Crepes*, page 3
1 tbs. vegetable oil
½ cup chopped onions
½ cup diced red bell peppers
1 large clove garlic, minced
½ cup cooked corn

½ tsp. ground cumin
1 cup nonfat refried beans
1 large tomato, peeled,
  seeded, chopped
½ cup grated cheddar cheese
½ cup fresh cilantro leaves for
  garnish

Make crepes. Preheat oven to 375°. Heat oil in a small skillet and sauté onions and peppers for 3 to 4 minutes until onions are soft and translucent. Add garlic, corn and cumin and cook for another minute. Stir in beans and heat through. Fill crepes with bean mixture, top beans with tomato pieces, roll up and place in a buttered ovenproof serving dish or individual serving dishes. Top with cheddar cheese and bake for 10 to 15 minutes until lightly browned and hot. Sprinkle with fresh cilantro leaves and serve.

Makes 3-4 servings

CURRIED EGG CREPES

Try these for breakfast, brunch or a light supper. Cranberry sauce or a mango chutney provides a perfect finishing touch.

8 *Whole Wheat Crepes,* page 13
2 tbs. butter
2 tsp. curry powder
2 tbs. flour
2 cups milk

salt and freshly ground pepper
6 hard-cooked eggs, chopped
chopped fresh cilantro for
 garnish

Make crepes. Melt butter in small saucepan. Add curry powder and flour and cook for 2 to 3 minutes. Gradually add milk, and cook, stirring, over low heat until sauce thickens. Season with salt and pepper. Stir 1/2 to 3/4 cup sauce into chopped eggs to moisten them. Divide egg filling among crepes. Roll and place in a buttered, ovenproof serving dish or individual dishes. Top with remaining sauce. Broil until lightly browned and bubbly. Sprinkle with cilantro and serve immediately.

Makes 4 servings

MANICOTTI

This is an easy Italian-style dish of cheese-filled crepes with a tomato sauce. If you wish, ½ cup sautéed sliced mushrooms can be added to the cheese filling.

8 *Manicotti Crepes*, page 14	1 egg
½ lb. mozzarella cheese, grated	½ cup diced ham
½ lb. ricotta cheese	1 can (15 oz) Italian-style tomato sauce
salt and freshly ground pepper	¼ cup grated Parmesan cheese

Make crepes. Preheat oven to 350°. Combine mozzarella, ricotta, salt, pepper, egg and ham. Spread filling down center of crepes. Roll and place seam-side down in an oiled ovenproof casserole or individual serving dishes. Top with tomato sauce and sprinkle with Parmesan cheese. Place in oven for about 15 minutes, or until hot and bubbly.

Makes 4 servings

INDIAN-STYLE CURRIED POTATO CREPES

*A curry-flavored potato and pea mixture makes a great entrée or side dish for roast pork or chicken. Serve with **Yogurt Cucumber Sauce**, page 47, or a fruit chutney.*

4-6 *Whole Wheat Crepes*, page 13, or *Buttermilk Crepes*, page 9
1 tbs. vegetable oil
1 cup chopped onions
1 small jalapeño pepper, seeds and veins removed, minced
1 tsp. curry powder
2 cups cooked potatoes, cut in ¾-inch cubes
2 tsp. lemon juice
½ cup water
1 cup cooked green peas, or defrosted frozen peas
2 tbs. butter

Make crepes. Heat oil in a medium skillet; cook onions and pepper until onions are soft and translucent. Add curry powder and cook for another minute. Add potatoes, lemon juice and water; stir

to combine. Bring to a simmer, cover and cook for 5 m
Remove cover and mash vegetables gently with the ba
spoon to make a spreadable mixture. Add peas and heat thro.
Stir in butter. Divide mixture among crepes and roll up or fold into
triangles. Place in a buttered ovenproof serving dish and broil until
lightly browned.

Makes 2-3 servings

YOGURT CUCUMBER SAUCE

1 cup plain yogurt
3 green onions, finely chopped
1 tsp. dried dill weed
1 tbs. rice wine vinegar
1 medium tomato, peeled,
  seeded, chopped

1 medium cucumber, peeled,
  seeded, coarsely grated,
  about 1 cup
salt and freshly ground pepper

Combine ingredients and pour into a serving bowl. Refrigerate for at least 1 hour before serving. Makes 1¾ cups.

CABBAGE-APPLE CREPES WITH LEMON SAUCE

This is a great vegetable entrée, or make smaller crepes and serve as an accompaniment to roast pork or chicken. Use the food processor to grate the vegetables.

10 *Classic Crepes*, page 3,
  or *Buttermilk Crepes*, page 9
2 tbs. vegetable oil
1 medium onion, chopped
½ medium head cabbage,
  1 lb. after trimming, coarsely
  grated
2 large carrots, peeled and
  coarsely grated

1 large tart apple, peeled,
  cored and coarsely grated
1 tsp. dried thyme
½ cup water, or white wine
salt and pepper
Lemon Sauce, page 49
fresh minced parsley for
  garnish

Make crepes. Heat oil in a large skillet and sauté onion for 3 to 4 minutes to soften. Add cabbage, carrots, apple and thyme to skillet. Toss to combine with onion. Add water, salt and pepper, bring to a boil, cover and cook over low heat for 10 minutes while

making sauce. Remove cover and cook over high heat until all moisture evaporates and mixture is lightly browned. Reserve ½ cup sauce for topping and mix remaining sauce into vegetables. Fill crepes, fold into triangles or roll up and place in a buttered ovenproof serving dish. Top with reserved sauce and broil until hot and lightly browned. Garnish with parsley.

Makes 4-5 servings

LEMON SAUCE

3 tbs. butter	2 tsp. sugar
3 tbs. flour	3 tbs. lemon juice
1½ cups milk	salt and freshly ground pepper

Melt butter in a small saucepan. Stir in flour and cook for 2 minutes. Add milk and sugar. Continue to cook, stirring, until mixture comes to a boil and thickens. Stir in lemon juice, salt and pepper. Makes 1½ cups.

'PINACH AND RICOTTA CHEESE CREPES

A marvelous blending of flavors — you'll want to enjoy it often.

8 *Whole Wheat Crepes*, page 13
1 pkg. (10 oz.) frozen chopped
  spinach, cooked and drained
1 tbs. butter
½ cup finely chopped onion
dash dried red pepper flakes
½ tsp. dried basil

½ tsp. dried thyme
1 cup ricotta cheese
⅓ cup grated Parmesan cheese
salt and freshly ground pepper
dash nutmeg
½ cup diced ham, or prosciutto
Cheese Sauce, page 51

Make crepes. Preheat oven to 375°. Drain and squeeze spinach until as dry as possible. Chop coarsely to break up strings. Melt butter in a medium skillet. Sauté onion, dried red pepper flakes, basil and thyme for 5 to 6 minutes until onion is soft but not brown. Add chopped spinach and cook for 1 to 2 minutes. Remove from heat; stir in ricotta, Parmesan cheese and remaining ingredients. Fill and roll crepes. Place in a buttered ovenproof serving dish or

individual au gratin dishes. Top with *Cheese Sauce*. Heat in oven for about 10 minutes until lightly browned and bubbly.

Makes 4 servings

CHEESE SAUCE

2 tbs. butter
2 tbs. flour
1¼ cups milk
½ tsp. Dijon mustard

1 tsp. Worcestershire sauce
⅓ cup grated Parmesan
  cheese
salt and white pepper

Melt butter in a small saucepan over medium heat. Add flour and cook, stirring, for 2 minutes. Gradually blend in milk. Cook, stirring, until sauce thickens. Add mustard, Worcestershire, cheese, salt and pepper. Heat through. Makes 1½ cups.

LAMB CREPES WITH PEPPERS AND GOAT CHEESE

Chunks of leftover barbecued lamb are paired with sweet onions and peppers, and served with a Middle Eastern-style sauce. Add a small peeled, chopped tomato to the sauce if you like. This is equally good made with beef or chicken.

8 *Spinach Crepes*, page 12, or *Whole Wheat Crepes*, page 13
$\frac{1}{4}$ cup fresh goat cheese, or cream cheese
2 tbs. full-flavored olive oil
1 medium onion, peeled and chopped
1 medium red pepper, cut into thin strips
$\frac{1}{2}$ tsp. ground cumin
dash cayenne pepper
salt and freshly ground pepper
2 cups cooked lamb, cut into $\frac{3}{4}$-inch chunks or strips
$\frac{1}{2}$ cup fresh cilantro leaves
Cumin Yogurt Sauce, page 53

Make crepes. Lightly spread crepes with goat cheese or cream cheese on one side. Preheat oven to 375°. Heat olive oil in a medium skillet; sauté onion and pepper for 8 to 10 minutes until vegetables are soft. Add cumin, cayenne, salt, pepper and lamb. Cook for 3 to 4 minutes to heat through. Divide lamb mixture among crepes. Sprinkle with fresh cilantro leaves, roll up and place in an oiled shallow ovenproof casserole or individual serving dishes. Heat in oven for 10 to 15 minutes. Spoon a dollop of *Cumin Yogurt Sauce* over crepes and serve immediately.

Makes 4 servings

CUMIN YOGURT SAUCE

1 cup plain yogurt
1 tsp. ground cumin
2 tbs. minced fresh cilantro leaves
2 tbs. chopped fresh mint

Combine ingredients. Makes 1 cup.

PROVENÇALE VEGETABLE CREPES

Fresh garden vegetables and herbs make a colorful and delicious filling for crepes.

8 *Classic Crepes*, page 3, or *Spinach Crepes*, page 12
2 tbs. full-flavored olive oil
6-8 medium mushrooms, thinly sliced
1 large onion, coarsely chopped
$\frac{1}{2}$ red bell pepper, cut into $\frac{3}{4}$-inch pieces
3 Japanese or Chinese eggplants, about $\frac{1}{2}$ lb., peeled, diced
3 large tomatoes, peeled, seeded, chopped
1 clove garlic, finely minced
2 tbs. chopped fresh basil
1 tsp. fresh thyme leaves
dash dried red pepper flakes
salt and freshly ground pepper
$\frac{1}{2}$ cup grated Romano or Parmesan cheese

Make crepes. Preheat oven to 375°. Heat olive oil in a large skillet. Sauté mushrooms over high heat for 2 to 3 minutes. Remove mushrooms to a plate. Add onion to skillet and cook for 3 to 4 minutes. Add pepper pieces and eggplants; cook for 3 to 4 minutes, and add tomatoes, garlic, herbs, pepper flakes, salt and pepper. Cover and cook over low heat for 10 to 15 minutes. Stir in mushrooms. If mixture isn't quite dry, raise heat and cook for 1 to 2 minutes to evaporate juices. Divide vegetables among crepes and sprinkle with half of the grated cheese. Roll up and place in an oiled ovenproof casserole. Sprinkle with remaining cheese. Bake for 10 to 15 minutes until hot.

Makes 4 servings

BASIC BLINTZES

Blintzes are specially folded crepes which are sautéed just before serving. Small blintzes make great appetizers.

3 eggs
1¼ cups milk
2 tbs. melted butter
1 cup all-purpose flour

½ tsp. salt
2 tsp. butter and 2 tsp.
   vegetable oil for frying

Place ingredients in a blender or food processor and blend on high speed for 20 to 30 seconds. Scrape down sides of bowl and blend for a few more seconds. Cook blintzes in a 7- to 8-inch crepe pan according to directions beginning on page 3, but cook until lightly browned on one side only. Place uncooked crepe side down and spoon filling on lightly browned side. See diagram on page 8 for filling and rolling blintzes. When ready to serve, heat butter and oil over medium heat in a large skillet. Sauté rolled blintzes for 3 to 4 minutes on each side until golden brown. Drain on paper towels and serve hot.

Makes 10-12 blintzes

CHICKEN AND ROASTED
RED PEPPER BLINTZES

This is a spicy nontraditional filling for blintzes. Serve with a fresh tomato salsa.

6 *Basic Blintzes*, page 56
⅓ cup finely chopped roasted
  red pepper, or pimiento pieces
2 cups diced cooked chicken,
  or turkey
3-4 tbs. sour cream

¼ cup fresh chopped cilantro
  leaves
salt and freshly ground pepper
2 tsp. butter and 2 tsp.
  vegetable oil for frying

Make blintz wrappers. Combine chopped pepper with chicken and enough sour cream just to moisten. Add seasonings. See diagram on page 8 for filling and rolling blintzes. When ready to serve, heat butter and oil in a large skillet. Sauté rolled blintzes for 2 to 3 minutes on each side until golden brown. Drain on paper towels and serve hot.

Makes 6 blintzes

BEEF BLINTZES

This is one of the classic meat fillings for blintzes. Ground turkey is an excellent substitute for beef.

6-8 *Basic Blintzes*, page 56
½ lb. lean ground beef
1 tbs. butter or vegetable oil
½ cup finely chopped onion
⅓ cup water
1 tsp. prepared mustard
½ tsp. prepared horseradish
2 tsp. Worcestershire sauce
salt and freshly ground pepper
2-3 tbs. sour cream
1 hard-cooked egg, finely chopped
2 tsp. butter and 2 tsp. vegetable oil for frying

Make blintz wrappers. Brown meat in a skillet, crumbling into small pieces. Drain and set aside. Pour fat from skillet and add butter or oil and onion. Cook over low heat for 3 to 4 minutes. Add ⅓ cup water and simmer for 3 to 4 minutes until onion is soft. Add meat, onion, mustard, horseradish, Worcestershire, salt and pepper. Cook until liquid evaporates. Remove from heat and allow to cool. Stir in sour cream and egg. See diagram on page 8 for filling and rolling blintzes. When ready to serve, heat butter and oil in a large skillet. Sauté rolled blintzes for 2 to 3 minutes on each side until golden brown. Drain on paper towels and serve hot.

Makes 6-8 large blintzes

TUNA BLINTZES

These savory blintzes make a delicious lunch or supper on a frosty day. Serve with a Waldorf or orange and onion salad.

6 *Basic Blintzes*, page 56
5-6 green onions, white part
  only, thinly sliced
2 tbs. finely minced celery
1 tbs. butter
1 can (6 oz.) tuna, drained

1 tsp. Dijon mustard
freshly ground pepper
½ cup grated cheddar cheese
2 tsp. butter and 2 tsp.
  vegetable oil for frying

Make blintz wrappers. Sauté onions and celery in butter for 3 to 4 minutes until soft. Stir in tuna, mustard, pepper and cheese. See diagram on page 8 for filling and rolling blintzes. When ready to serve, heat butter and oil in a large skillet. Sauté blintzes for 2 to 3 minutes on each side until golden brown. Drain on paper towels and serve hot.

Makes 6 blintzes

COCKTAIL-SIZED MUSHROOM BLINTZES

Make these savory blintzes ahead and fry just before serving.

12 *Basic Blintzes* (5-inch),
  page 56
1 tbs. butter
1/4 cup finely chopped onions
1/2 lb. mushrooms, finely
  chopped

1/4 tsp. dried tarragon
salt and freshly ground pepper
1/4 cup fresh goat cheese, or
  cream cheese
2 tsp. butter and 2 tsp.
  vegetable oil for frying

Make blintz wrappers. Melt butter in a medium skillet and sauté onions over low heat for 5 to 6 minutes until very soft. Turn up heat and sauté mushrooms for 3 to 4 minutes until mixture is very dry. Season with tarragon, salt and pepper while cooking mushrooms. Remove from heat and allow to cool almost to room temperature before stirring in goat cheese. See diagram on page 8 for filling and rolling blintzes. When ready to serve, heat butter and oil in a large skillet. Sauté rolled blintzes for 2 to 3 minutes on each side until golden brown. Drain on paper towels and serve hot.

Makes 12 blintzes

CHEESE DESSERT BLINTZES

This is another classic filling that you can vary by adding ½ cup drained cooked apples, cherries or blueberries.

6 *Basic Blintzes*, page 56
1 cup small curd creamed
   cottage cheese
1 pkg. (3 oz.) cream cheese
¼ cup sour cream
3 tbs. sugar

½ tsp. grated lemon rind
2 tsp. butter and 2 tsp.
   vegetable oil for frying
½ cup cooked fruit, optional
sour cream, optional

Make blintz wrappers. Place cottage cheese, cream cheese, sour cream, sugar and lemon rind in a food processor and process until mixture is smooth and creamy. Add cooked fruit if desired. See diagram on page 8 for filling and rolling blintzes. When ready to serve, heat butter and oil in a large skillet. Sauté filled blintzes for 2 to 3 minutes on each side until golden brown. Drain on paper towels and serve hot. Serve extra sour cream if desired.

Makes 6 blintzes

BANANA CREAM CREPES

Make the custard ahead and assemble just before serving.

12 dessert crepes, any kind
3 tbs. all-purpose flour
⅓ cup sugar
4 tsp. cornstarch
dash salt
2 cups milk

2 egg yolks, lightly beaten
1 tbs. butter
1½ tsp. vanilla extract
1 large or 2 small bananas,
  diced
superfine sugar

Make crepes. Combine flour, sugar, cornstarch and salt in a small saucepan. Add milk gradually. Cook, stirring, over low heat until mixture thickens. Blend a little hot mixture into egg yolks and carefully stir back into sauce. Cook over low heat for another minute. Remove from heat, add vanilla and butter, and allow to cool. When ready to serve, fold in diced bananas. Fill and roll crepes. Place in a buttered ovenproof serving dish or individual serving dishes. Sprinkle crepes with superfine sugar. Broil for 2 to 3 minutes until slightly warm and edges are lightly browned.

Makes 6 servings

CHERRY-SAUCED CREPES

This is a delicious sauce just spooned over plain, warm crepes, or serve as a topping for crepes with a vanilla ice cream or whipped cream filling.

1 can (17 oz.) pitted dark sweet cherries
2 tbs. sugar
$\frac{1}{8}$ tsp. lemon extract
2 tsp. cornstarch
2 tbs. cold water
1 tbs. Kirsch, or brandy

Drain juice from cherries into a small saucepan. Set cherries aside. Add sugar and lemon extract to cherry juice. Cook over low heat until sugar dissolves. Mix cornstarch with water and add to juice. Cook, stirring constantly, until sauce boils and thickens. Remove from heat. Add Kirsch and cherries. Serve warm or cold.

Makes 2 cups

CHESTNUT RUM CREPES

*Use this filling in **Chocolate** or **Classic Dessert Crepes** and top with chocolate shavings for an elegant party or holiday dessert.*

12 *Chocolate Crepes*, page 16,
  or *Classic Dessert Crepes*,
  page 15
1 cup heavy cream
2 tbs. sugar

3 tbs. rum or brandy
1 can (8¾ oz.) sweetened
  chestnut puree
chocolate shavings for garnish

Make crepes. Whip cream with sugar until stiff peaks form. Stir rum or brandy into chestnut puree. Fold whipped cream into chestnut puree. Fill and roll crepes, reserving about 6 tbs. filling to garnish crepes. Place 2 crepes on each serving plate. Spoon a little reserved filling on plate and sprinkle crepes with chocolate shavings.

Servings: 6

CREPES MELBA

Make sliced peach- and cream-filled crepes topped with raspberry sauce when fresh peaches are in season.

8 *Classic Dessert Crepes*, page 15
½ cup whipping cream
¼ cup sugar
½ cup ricotta cheese
1 cup fresh raspberries

¼ cup sugar
2 tbs. Triple Sec, Kirsch or orange juice
2-3 fresh ripe peaches, peeled and thinly sliced

Make crepes. Whip cream until soft peaks form, add ¼ cup sugar and beat until stiff. Fold whipped cream into ricotta cheese. Puree fresh raspberries in blender and push through a strainer to remove seeds. Add ¼ cup sugar and Triple Sec to raspberry puree. Heat raspberry sauce in a microwave or a small saucepan just before serving. When ready to fill crepes, add peaches to whipped cream and ricotta mixture and spoon into crepes. Roll up and place filled crepes on dessert plates. Spoon warm raspberry sauce over crepes.

Makes 4 servings

MEXICAN CHOCOLATE-SAUCED CREPES

This cinnamon orange chocolate sauce is great paired with whipped cream- or ice cream-filled crepes. Make it ahead, refrigerate, and reheat in the microwave to serve.

8 *Classic Dessert Crepes*,
  page 15
1 round (8 wedges) Ibarra
  Mexican chocolate, cut into
  small pieces

1 cup heavy cream
½ cup heavy cream
1 tbs. brandy, or dark rum

Make crepes. Heat chocolate and ½ cup heavy cream together over low heat until chocolate melts and mixture is smooth and creamy; stir in brandy. Spread a thin layer of chocolate sauce over each crepe, top with a little whipped cream and roll up crepes tightly. To serve, place crepe in a buttered, ovenproof serving dish. Top with remaining chocolate sauce and broil for 1 to 2 minutes to warm. Top with remaining whipped cream and serve immediately.

Makes 4 servings

CREPES SUZETTE

Prepare and flame this elegant dessert at the table for your guests.

12 *Orange Dessert Crepes*, page 17
½ cup butter
2 tbs. frozen orange juice concentrate, undiluted
2 tbs. sugar
1 tbs. Triple Sec, or orange liqueur
grated orange rind from 1 orange
1 tbs. sugar
2 oz. brandy
1 oz. Triple Sec

Make crepes. Cream butter in a mixer bowl and gradually beat in orange juice, sugar, Triple Sec and orange rind. Beat until most of liquid has been absorbed by butter. When ready to serve crepes, add orange butter to a large crepe suzette pan or skillet over low heat. If cooking at the table, stack crepes on a plate nearby. Pick

up one crepe, using a fork in one hand and a tablespoon in the other. (In the kitchen without an audience, fingers work well.) Place crepe in melted orange butter and quickly turn to coat other side. Fold in half and then fold again. Push to one side of pan and repeat with another crepe. When all crepes have been coated and folded, arrange in a single layer in pan, overlapping as necessary. Sprinkle with 1 tbs. sugar. Combine brandy and Triple Sec and pour over folded crepes. Allow to heat for a few seconds. Light with a long match, averting your face and holding hand away from pan. Spoon flaming sauce over crepes and serve as soon as flames die. If preparing crepes in the kitchen, carry flaming pan to the table and serve 2 to 3 crepes per person.

Makes 4-6 servings

CREAMY CHOCOLATE-FILLED CREPES

This is delicious in chocolate or orange dessert crepes.

8 *Sour Cream Dessert Crepes,*
  page 18
1 cup milk
1 oz. bitter chocolate
½ oz. semisweet chocolate
⅓ cup sugar

2 tsp. cornstarch dissolved in
  1 tbs. dark rum and 1 tsp. water
1 tsp. vanilla extract
dash salt
1 cup heavy cream, whipped

Make crepes and set aside. Place milk, chocolates and sugar in a small saucepan over low heat until chocolate melts. Add dissolved cornstarch-rum mixture and cook, stirring, until sauce thickens and becomes very smooth. Stir in vanilla and salt. Cool. Spread a small amount of chocolate filling on each crepe. Spread chocolate with some whipped cream and roll up crepes. Top with whipped cream and serve slightly warm. Or, place in a buttered ovenproof dish without whipped cream topping and broil for 1 to 2 minutes to heat. Top with whipped cream and serve immediately.

Makes 4 servings

HONEY SHERRY TRIANGLES

*This topping is delicious with **Walnut Crepes**, page 19. Serve with a small glass of cream sherry for a special dessert.*

8 *Walnut Dessert Crepes*,
  page 19
3 tbs. butter
½ cup sweet cream sherry

3 tbs. honey
1½ tsp. lemon juice
whipped cream or vanilla ice
  cream for topping

Make crepes. Melt butter in small saucepan. Add sherry, honey and lemon juice; bring to a boil. Cook for 2 to 3 minutes until mixture thickens slightly and alcohol has boiled off. Dip both sides of crepes in this mixture. Fold crepes into triangles and place in a buttered ovenproof serving dish or individual serving dishes. Pour remaining sauce over crepes. Broil until crepes are heated through and lightly browned on edges. Serve with a dollop of whipped cream or a little vanilla ice cream.

Makes 4 servings

JAM OR JELLY CREPES

This is a quick and easy way to satisfy a sweet tooth, and it looks elegant. Allow 2 to 3 triangles per person.

FOR EACH DESSERT CREPE:

1-2 tsp. favorite jelly, jam or marmalade
superfine sugar
brandy
whipped cream, slightly sweetened
1-2 tsp. chopped nuts

Spread crepe with jelly or jam. Fold in half and fold again, making a triangle. Place in a buttered, ovenproof serving dish or individual serving dishes. Sprinkle with sugar and a few drops brandy. Broil to heat and lightly brown. Top with whipped cream and chopped nuts. Serve immediately.

LEMON MERINGUE CREPES

This is for lemon lovers. Make the crepe filling ahead of ti

8 dessert crepes
2 eggs, separated
½ cup sugar
2 tbs. flour
¼ cup lemon juice

¾ cup milk
grated rind from 1 lemon
⅛ tsp. lemon extract
2 tbs. sugar

Make crepes. Preheat oven to 450°. Beat egg yolks with ½ cup sugar until thick and lemon-colored. Add flour and lemon juice. Mix well. Heat milk in a small saucepan. Carefully combine with egg yolks and cook, stirring, over low heat until sauce thickens. Remove from heat. Pour through a strainer into a bowl. Add lemon rind and lemon extract and allow mixture to cool. Just before serving, beat egg whites with 2 tbs. sugar until stiff peaks form. Fill crepes with lemon filling. Roll and place in 4 buttered ovenproof individual serving dishes. Top with meringue. Heat in oven for 5 minutes, or until meringue is lightly browned. Serve immediately.

Servings: 4

BRANDIED FRESH FIG CREPES

Sautéed fresh ripe figs make a terrific crepe filling. Increase the recipe to meet the demand.

4 *Classic Dessert Crepes,*
  page 15
1 tbs. butter
4 fresh ripe figs

1 tbs. sugar
2 tbs. brandy, or cognac
¼ cup heavy cream

Make crepes. Trim ends from figs and cut into quarters. Melt butter in a small skillet and add figs, cut side up. Cook over low heat for 2 to 3 minutes until lightly browned on one side. Turn over and sprinkle with sugar. Cook for 2 to 3 minutes until sugar melts. Add brandy and carefully flame, averting face. Cook until sauce is a light caramel color. Stir occasionally to keep fruit from sticking. Stir in cream and heat through. Divide figs among crepes, placing them on one-quarter of crepe. Fold over crepe, and fold again, making a triangle (see illustration on page 8). Pour remaining brandy cream sauce over crepes and serve immediately.

Makes 2 servings

INDEX